KU-863-046

I didn't know that some trains run on water

ROTHERHAM LIBRARY &
INFORMATION SERVICES

J 625

783 078 4

R0 000406 2

SCHOOLS STOCK

© Aladdin Books Ltd 1997
Produced by
Aladdin Books Ltd
28 Percy Street
London W1P 0LD

ISBN 0-7496-2888-X

First published in Great Britain in 1997 by
Aladdin Books/Watts Books
96 Leonard Street
London EC2A 4RH

Concept, editorial and design by

David West 🧍🧍 Children's Books

Illustrators: Ross Watton, Jo Moore

Printed in Belgium

All rights reserved
A CIP catalogue record for this book is available from
the British Library

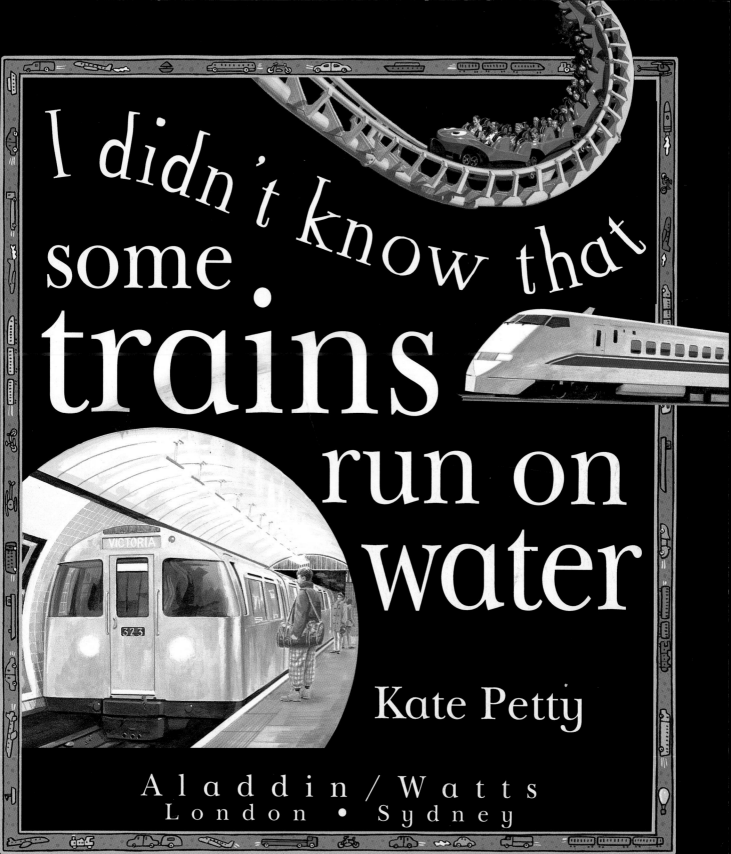

I didn't know that some trains run on water

Kate Petty

A l a d d i n / W a t t s
L o n d o n • S y d n e y

I didn't know that

Introduction

Did *you* know that trains opened up the American West? ... that they can have several locomotives? ... that they can go upside down?

Discover for yourself amazing facts about rail transport, from the earliest steam trains to the latest technology of the high-speed supertrains.

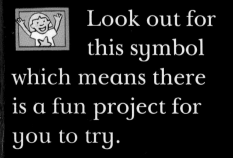
Look out for this symbol which means there is a fun project for you to try.

Is it true or is it false? Watch for this symbol and try to answer the question before reading on for the answer.

Don't forget to check the borders for extra amazing facts.

I didn't know that

the first steam trains went slower than walking pace.

In 1804, Richard Trevithick's steam engine pulled ten tons of iron ore and 70 passengers over 15 km. It took four hours and five minutes. Trevithick walked ahead all the way.

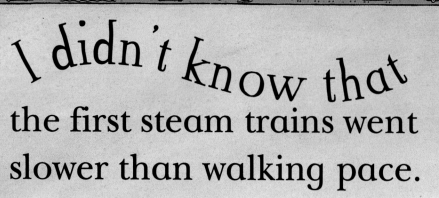

Can you find the running boy?

In 1829, *Rocket*, built by George Stephenson, won a competition for the best steam engine. It had an average speed of 20 km/h and a top speed of 47 km/h.

In 1808, *Catch Me Who Can* carried paying passengers.

True or false?
Horses pulled the first railway trains for passengers.

Answer: **True**
Nearly 200 years ago passengers were pulled by horses on the world's first passenger line in Wales. The Emperor and Empress of Austria used this form of transport 25 years later (above left).

I didn't know that

steam trains run on water.

A steam locomotive uses water to make its power. A coal fire heats the water until it turns to steam. The steam is forced into the *cylinders* where *pistons* are pushed to turn the drive wheels.

SEARCH & FIND
Follow the blue arrows to find where the water goes.

Boiler

Smoke stack

Drive wheels

Pistons inside cylinder

Blast pipes

HIAWATHA
STEAM LOCOMOTIVE

Trains can't always carry enough fuel so on long journeys they have to stop to take on more fuel and water.

Tender

Water

Driver

Coal

Firebox

Fireman

As well as the driver who controls the speed, reads the signals and stops and starts the train, each locomotive needs a fireman to tend the boiler. It is his job to stoke up the fire in the firebox and to keep the boiler well supplied with water.

Railways come in many different widths, or *gauges.*

I didn't know that

steam trains opened up the American West. By 1850 American railway companies had bought land and laid tracks from coast to coast. At last goods could get from factories in the east to the new towns in the west.

Sparks from the fire cool down and are kept safe in the tall smoke stack.

SEARCH & FIND

Can you find the three train robbers?

FIND & SEARCH

Before steam trains settlers travelled in wagon trains.

The first trains in America were sometimes known as 'Iron horses'.

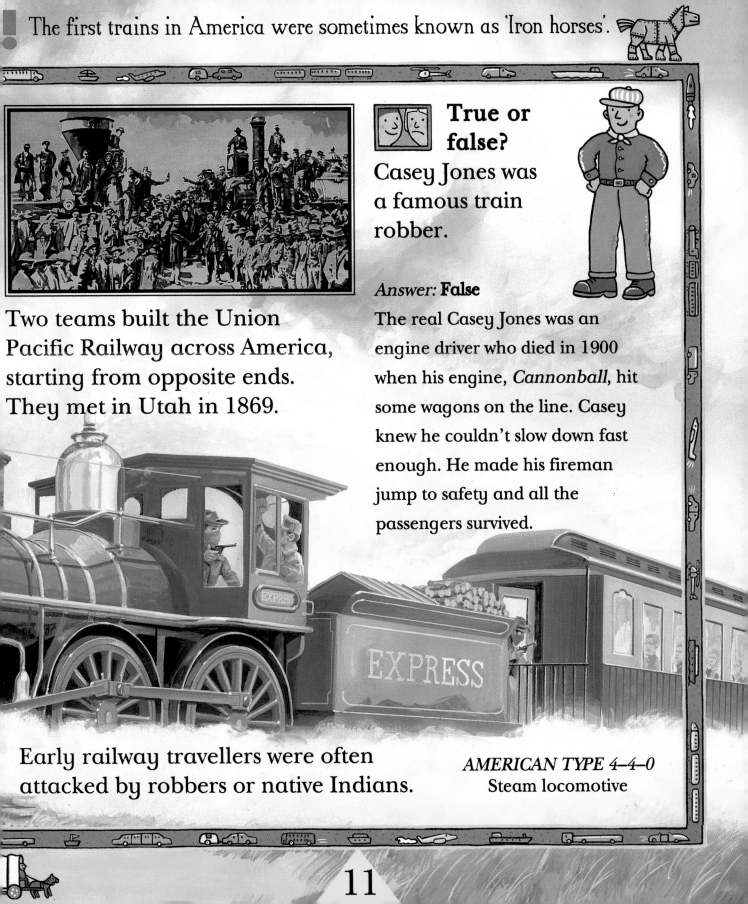

Two teams built the Union Pacific Railway across America, starting from opposite ends. They met in Utah in 1869.

True or false?

Casey Jones was a famous train robber.

Answer: **False**

The real Casey Jones was an engine driver who died in 1900 when his engine, *Cannonball*, hit some wagons on the line. Casey knew he couldn't slow down fast enough. He made his fireman jump to safety and all the passengers survived.

Early railway travellers were often attacked by robbers or native Indians.

AMERICAN TYPE 4–4–0
Steam locomotive

Wheel codes are the numbers used to describe an engine's *wheel combination*. The 2-6-2 on the left has 2 leading wheels, 6 driving wheels and 2 trailing wheels. Can you work out the wheel codes for A, B, C and D.

2 - 6 - 2

A   B   C   D

Answers: **A** 0-4-0 **B** 2-6-0 **C** 4-6-4 **D** 2-8-2

UNION PACIFIC   4019

Mallard was a famous streamlined British steam engine. It set the steam speed record of 203 km/h in 1938. This record has never been broken since!

MALLARD   N° 4468

One of the longest trains ever pulled 500 wagons of coal.

I didn't know that

the biggest steam locomotive had 24 wheels. The *Big Boy* hauled freight trains on the Union Pacific in the 1940s. This enormous *articulated* loco was nearly 40 metres long.

This is the 1866 steam locomotive, *Peppersass*. It pushed carriages up mountains. The wheels and rails were both 'toothed' (called *rack and pinion*) so they could grip each other.

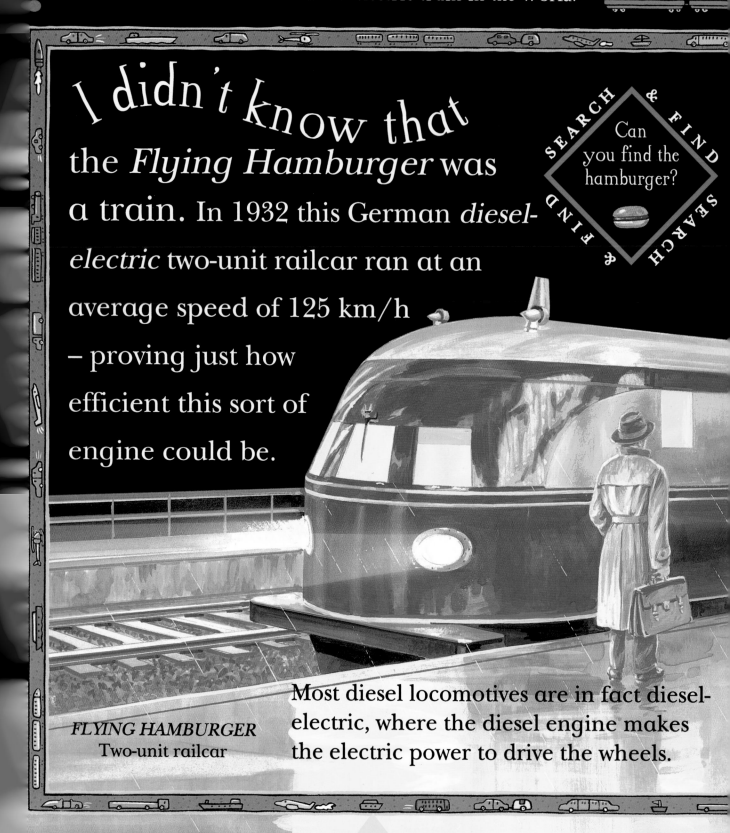

I didn't know that

the *Flying Hamburger* was a train. In 1932 this German *diesel-electric* two-unit railcar ran at an average speed of 125 km/h – proving just how efficient this sort of engine could be.

SEARCH & FIND
Can you find the hamburger?
FIND & SEARCH

FLYING HAMBURGER
Two-unit railcar

Most diesel locomotives are in fact diesel-electric, where the diesel engine makes the electric power to drive the wheels.

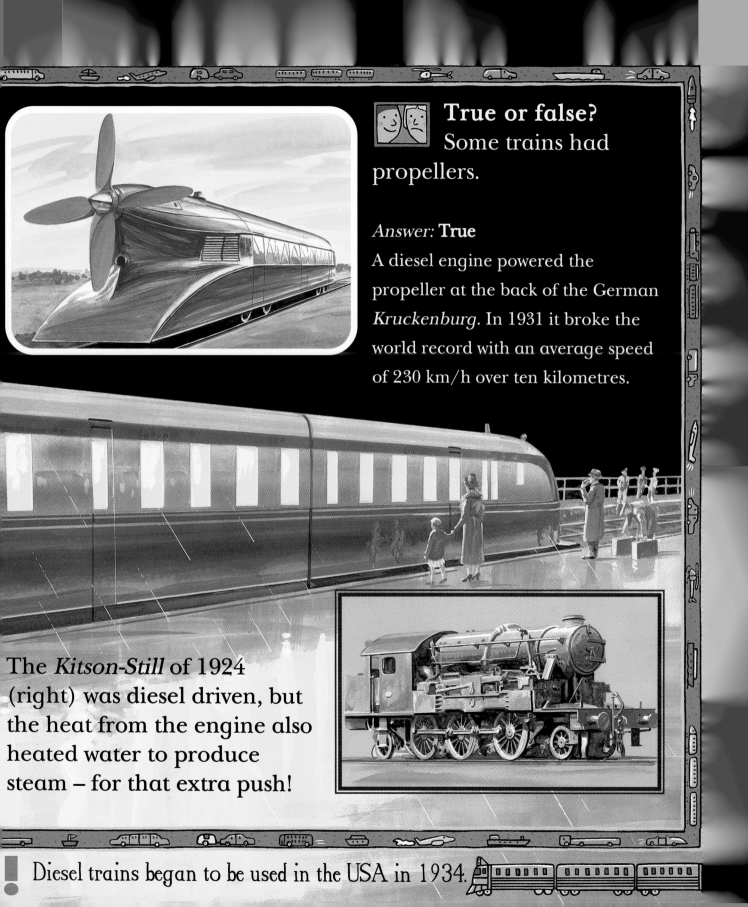

True or false?
Some trains had propellers.

Answer: **True**
A diesel engine powered the propeller at the back of the German *Kruckenburg*. In 1931 it broke the world record with an average speed of 230 km/h over ten kilometres.

The *Kitson-Still* of 1924 (right) was diesel driven, but the heat from the engine also heated water to produce steam – for that extra push!

Diesel trains began to be used in the USA in 1934.

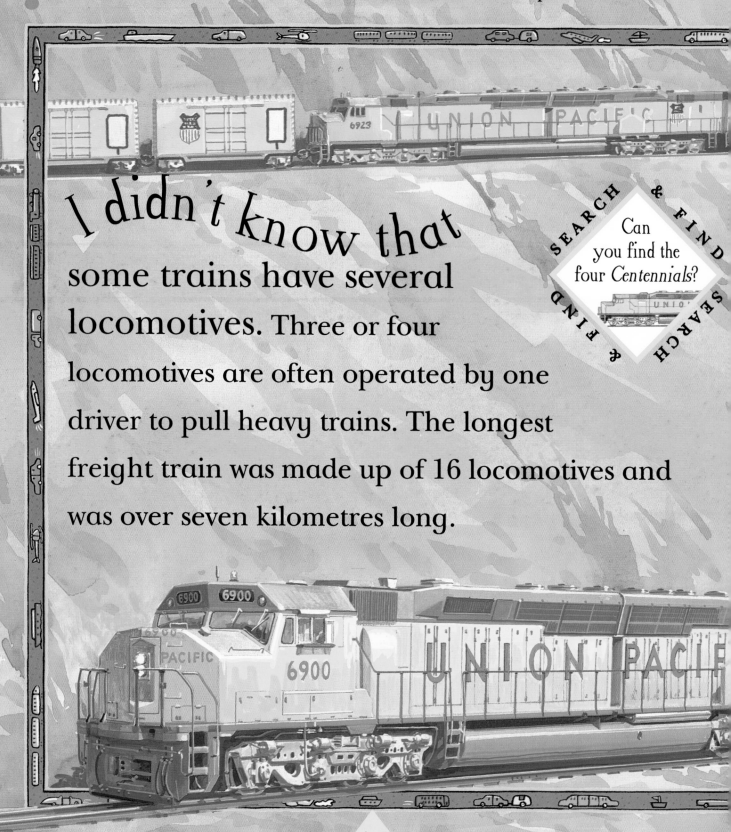

I didn't know that

some trains have several locomotives. Three or four locomotives are often operated by one driver to pull heavy trains. The longest freight train was made up of 16 locomotives and was over seven kilometres long.

SEARCH & FIND

Can you find the four *Centennials*?

FIND & SEARCH

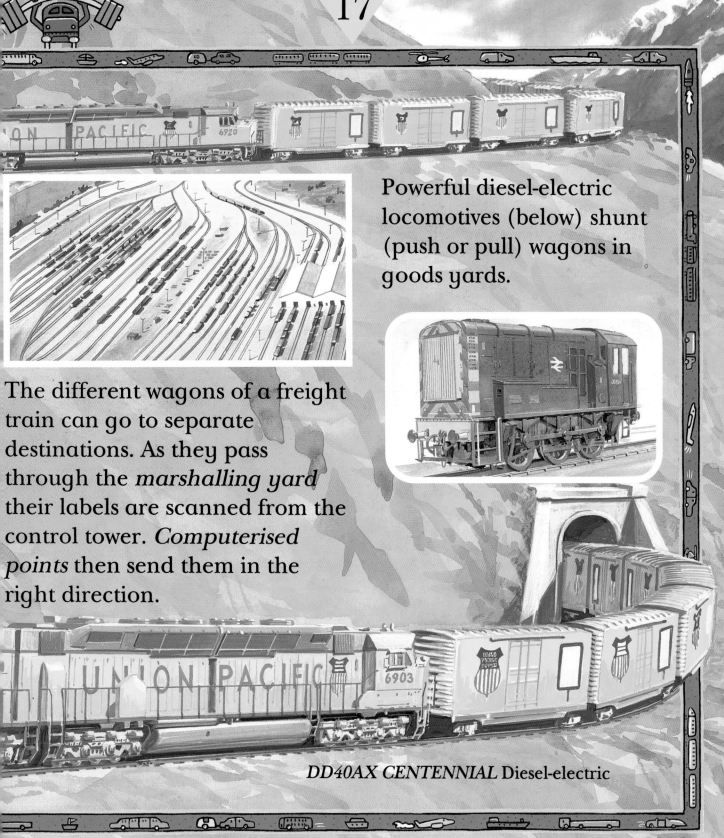

Powerful diesel-electric locomotives (below) shunt (push or pull) wagons in goods yards.

The different wagons of a freight train can go to separate destinations. As they pass through the *marshalling yard* their labels are scanned from the control tower. *Computerised points* then send them in the right direction.

DD40AX CENTENNIAL Diesel-electric

Union Pacific celebrated their 100 years with the new *Centennial* 100

I didn't know that

some trains don't make their own power. Some electric trains get their power from overhead wires via a metal *pantograph* on the roof, others from a *conductor rail* on the ground.

SEARCH & FIND
Can you find the steam engine?
FIND SEARCH &

BB-12005

S.N.C.F.

In 1883 Britain's first electric railway ran along Brighton seafront. It still doe

The *Regio Runners* in Holland (right) are double-decker intercity trains, powered from overhead electric wires.

French
CLASS 12000
Electric locomotive

True or false?

There were electric trains more than one hundred years ago.

Answer: **True**

Werner von Siemens (below) gave a demonstration of his electric locomotive in Berlin in 1879.

True or false?

Some trains don't need drivers.

Answer: **True**

The Docklands Light Railway (DLR right) in London and the Bay Area Rapid Transit system (BART) that runs under San Francisco Bay in America are operated from control centres by computers. A supervisor travels on board the DLR in case anything goes wrong.

SEARCH & FIND
Can you find four mice?
FIND & SEARCH

VICTORIA

323

I didn't know that

trains run beneath the city.

The oldest (1863) and biggest underground system is in London. Underground railways are now used all over the world.

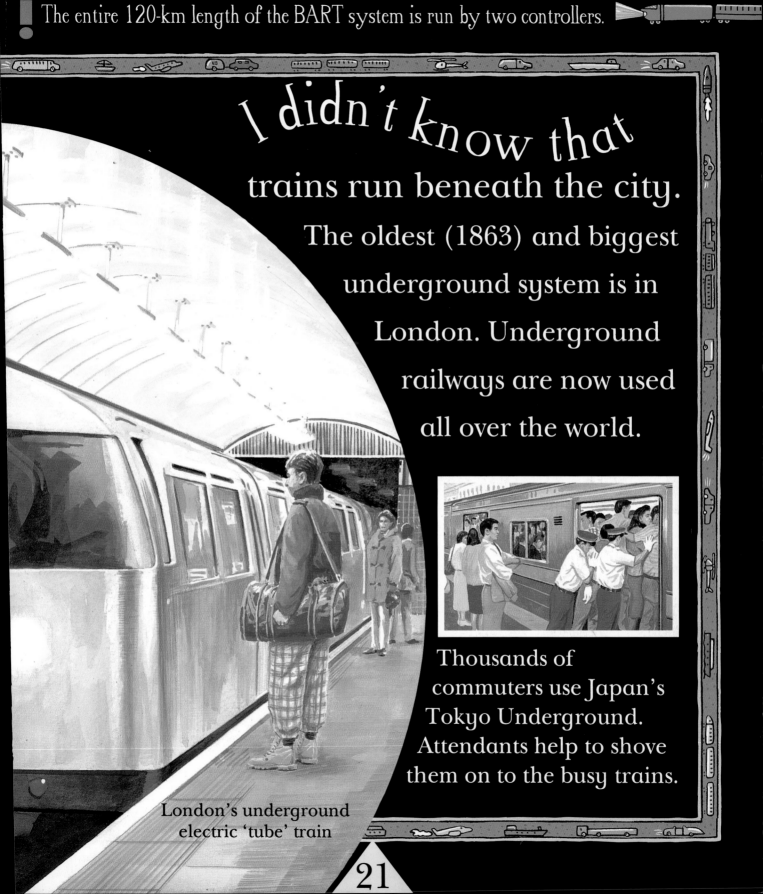

Thousands of commuters use Japan's Tokyo Underground. Attendants help to shove them on to the busy trains.

London's underground electric 'tube' train

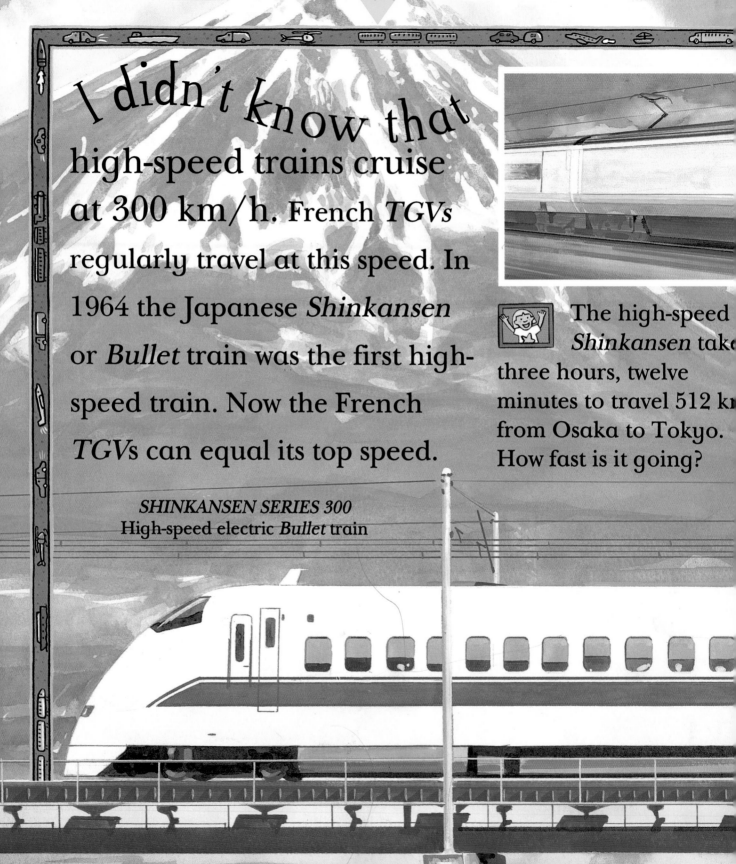

I didn't know that

high-speed trains cruise at 300 km/h. French *TGVs* regularly travel at this speed. In 1964 the Japanese *Shinkansen* or *Bullet* train was the first high-speed train. Now the French *TGVs* can equal its top speed.

The high-speed *Shinkansen* take three hours, twelve minutes to travel 512 k from Osaka to Tokyo. How fast is it going?

SHINKANSEN SERIES 300
High-speed electric *Bullet* train

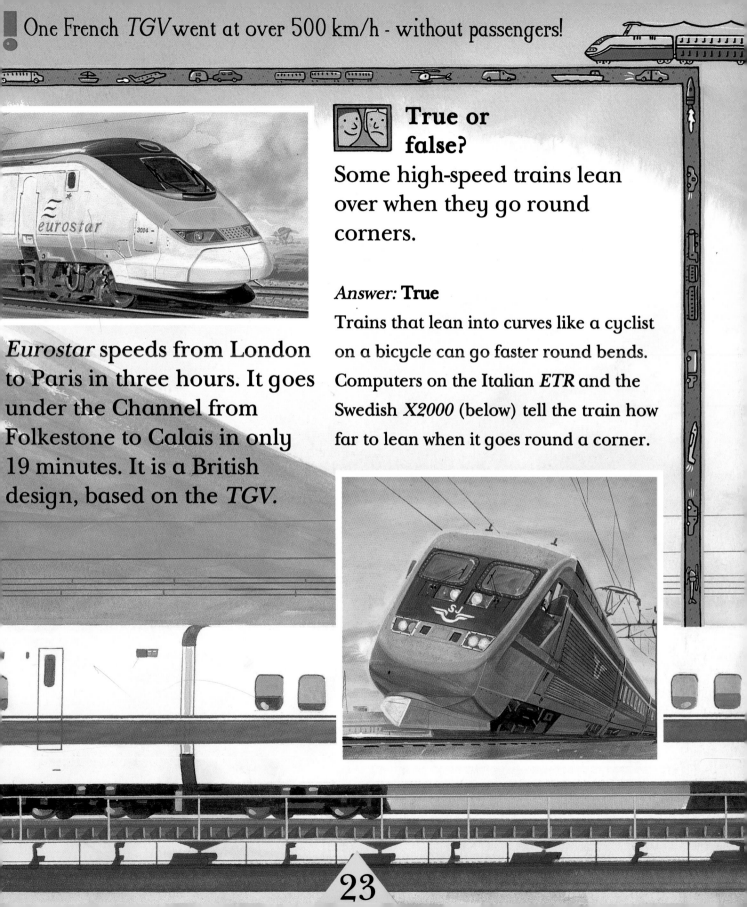

True or false?

Some high-speed trains lean over when they go round corners.

Answer: **True**

Trains that lean into curves like a cyclist on a bicycle can go faster round bends. Computers on the Italian *ETR* and the Swedish *X2000* (below) tell the train how far to lean when it goes round a corner.

Eurostar speeds from London to Paris in three hours. It goes under the Channel from Folkestone to Calais in only 19 minutes. It is a British design, based on the *TGV*.

I didn't know that

some trains run on only one rail. A *monorail* train rides either above or below a single rail. Two vertical wheels guide it along the track and horizontal wheels grip the sides. Sydney's monorail is built on stilts.

The Ballybunion Line in Ireland was a monorail system from 1888-1924. Invented by a Frenchman, Charles Lartigue, the double engine rode on an A-shaped line.

A train with no wheels! *TACV* stands for tracked air cushion vehicle – a hovercraft on rails. This experimental *Aerotrain* is powered by a jet plane's engine.

The power of electro-magnets can lift a train above the tracks so that it runs without friction, like this *Maglev* train. If you experiment with two ordinary magnets you will discover just how strong their pulls (attraction) and pushes (repulsion) can be.

A *MAGLEV* in Birmingham, England

Sydney, Australia's AEG von Roll monorail

JUST $6 IT'S SO EASY

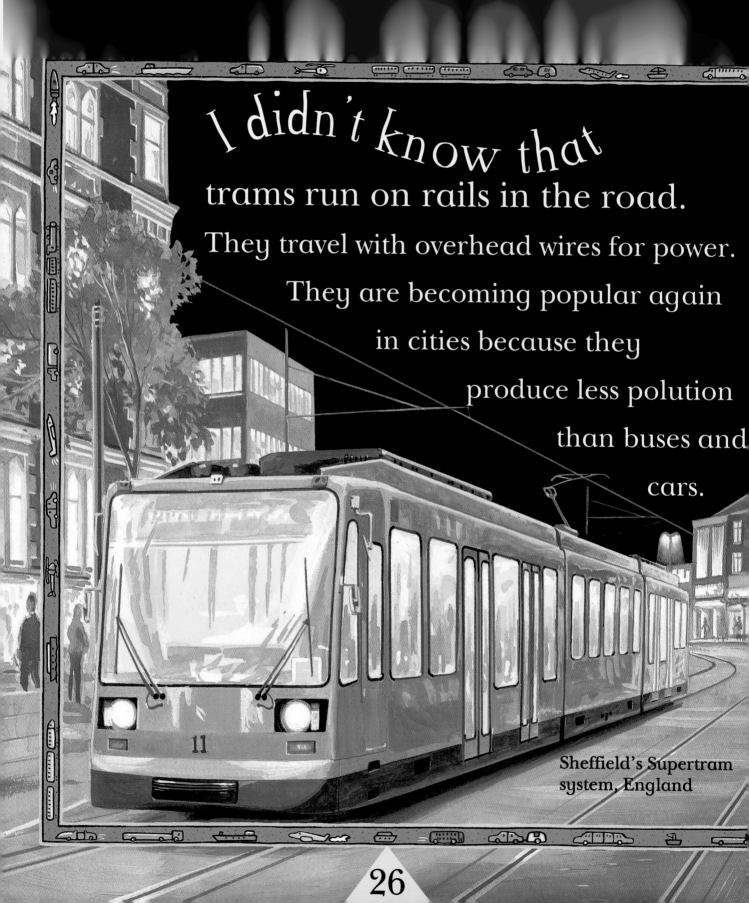

I didn't know that

trams run on rails in the road. They travel with overhead wires for power. They are becoming popular again in cities because they produce less polution than buses and cars.

Sheffield's Supertram system, England

Not all trains look like trains. This railcar, built in 1932 for the County Donegal Joint Railways in Ireland, looks much more like a bus!

 True or false?

The cars on a *cable railway* have electric motors.

Answer: **False**

The famous cable cars in San Francisco are pulled along by a moving loop of steel cable. The cable runs along a slot in between the rails and the cars clamp on to it.

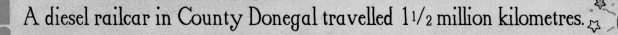
A diesel railcar in County Donegal travelled 1 1/2 million kilometres.

I didn't know that

some trains run upside down. Rollercoasters are scary but not dangerous. Speed and gravity hold them safely in place. Many also have hooks around the rails to help secure them.

Have a whole rail network in your own room! Most models are replicas of full-size trains. They are usually electric.

28

Can you find the ice cream?

True or false?

Some miniature trains carry passengers.

Answer: **True**

You can visit real miniature railways and even ride on some of them. This one is steam powered and is one-fifth the size of the original it has been copied from.

Glossary

Articulated
Built in connected sections. Helps long vehicles to go round bends more easily.

Cable railway
A railway where passenger cars are pulled along by a moving cable, operated by a stationary motor.

Computerised
Any system that is controlled by computers.

Conductor rail
Electrified rail that passes electricity to an electric train.

Cylinder
Wide tube in which gas expands to push a piston.

Diesel-electric
On diesel-electric trains the diesel engine powers a generator that provides electricity for the motor.

Gauge
The distance between the two rails on a railway track.

Maglev
Short for 'magnetic levitation'. A train that is moved and lifted along above the track by magnetic forces.

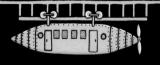

Marshalling yard

A place where freight wagons are shunted to make up trains.

Monorail

Railcars that run on a single rail.

Pantographs

The metal frames on top of an electric train that pick up the electric current from overhead wires.

Piston

The disc that moves inside the cylinder, attached to a rod that turns a crankshaft or flywheel.

Points

A junction where rails can be moved to send a train in a different direction.

Rack and pinion

A system of notched wheels and rails used on mountain railways.

TACV

Tracked Air Cushion Vehicle – one that moves on a cushion of air above a track.

Wheel combination

The way in which a locomotive's leading (front), driving and trailing (back) wheels are arranged.

Index

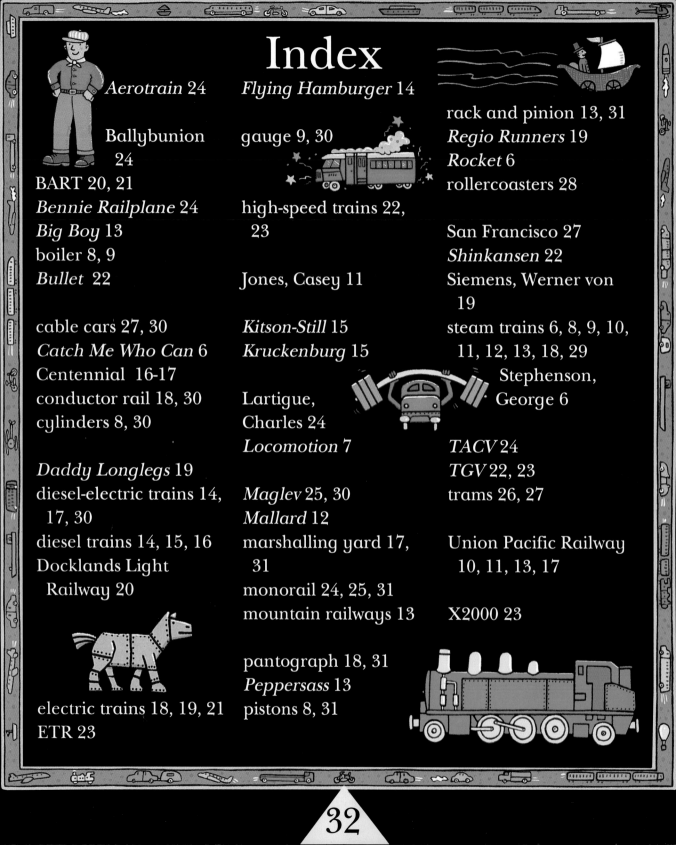